QUICK REFERENCE GUIDES

by Virginia Dooley

New York ❀ Toronto ❀ London ❀ Auckland ❀ Sydney

Mexico City ❀ New Delhi ❀ Hong Kong ❀ Buenos Aires

ISBN: 0-590-76994-4

Cover design by James Sarfati
Interior design by Grafica
Interior Illustrations by Mike Moran and Teresa Southwell

TABLE OF CONTENTS

Introduction 5

Spelling 11

Poetry 15

Literary Elements 19

Vocabulary 23

Writing 27

Grammar 31

Geography 37

U.S. History 41

Math 47

Science 51

Blank Template 55

Welcome to Quick Reference Guides!

About This Book

The ten, easy-to-make mini-books in this collection will give your students access to important information, rules, rubrics, and much more.

You may want to have students keep the books in their desks or folders, so they'll have the resources they need right at their fingertips. You may also want them to keep a set of the reference guides at home to help them with homework assignments.

We hope this collection of reference guides will give your students the tools they need to grow as independent learners.

How to Make the Quick Reference Guides

1. Carefully tear along the perforation at the left-hand margin to remove the pages you want to use.

2. Make a double-sided copy* of each page in the guide (one per student).

3. Have students cut the pages along the dashed lines.

4. Help students assemble the mini-book pages in order and then fold each piece along the solid center line.

5. Staple the books together along the folded edge.

6. You may want to have students place tape over the staples so they don't get scratched.

It might be helpful for you to model how to make one of the guides. Alternatively, you can invite parent volunteers to make the books for students.

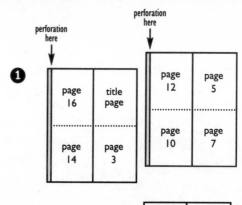

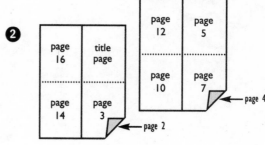

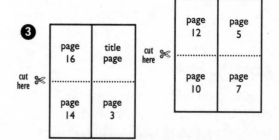

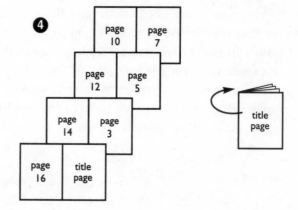

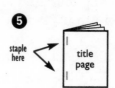

NOTE: If your photocopy machine does not have a double-sided function, follow these directions:

1. Make copies of the first full page of the mini-book pages (one per student).

2. Place the copies in the paper tray with the blank side facing up.

3. Make a copy of the second full page of the mini-book pages.

4. Make a test copy to be sure the pages are aligned correctly and that mini-book page 2 appears directly behind mini-book page 1.

5. Repeat these steps with the rest of the mini-book pages.

Using the Quick Reference Guides

Encourage students to color the illustrations where appropriate, e.g., the maps in the "Pocket Guide to Geography" or the illustrations in the "Pocket Guide to Science." Students may also want to annotate or underline information in their guides to highlight information on which they need to focus. Suggest that they make two copies of each book—one to use in class and the other to keep at home. The books can be stored in folders or they can be hole-punched and placed in a binder. Some of the guides include graphic organizers. Remind students to copy the organizers onto a larger piece of paper so that they are easier to write on.

Consider making and laminating a class set of Quick Reference Guides. A 3 1/2-inch diskette box makes a perfect storage container (cut off the top lid and tabs). You can use the template on page 8 to create a cover for the box. Cut out the template along the dashed lines and fold it along the solid lines. Tape the template to the box so that the section labeled "front" is positioned on the front of the box.

A blank pocket guide template is found on page 55.

Storage Box Cover

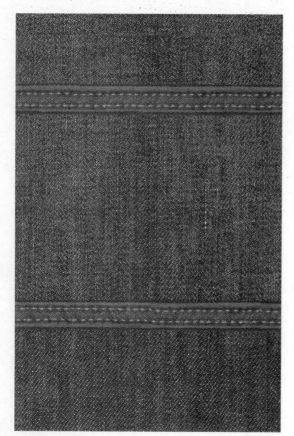

back cover

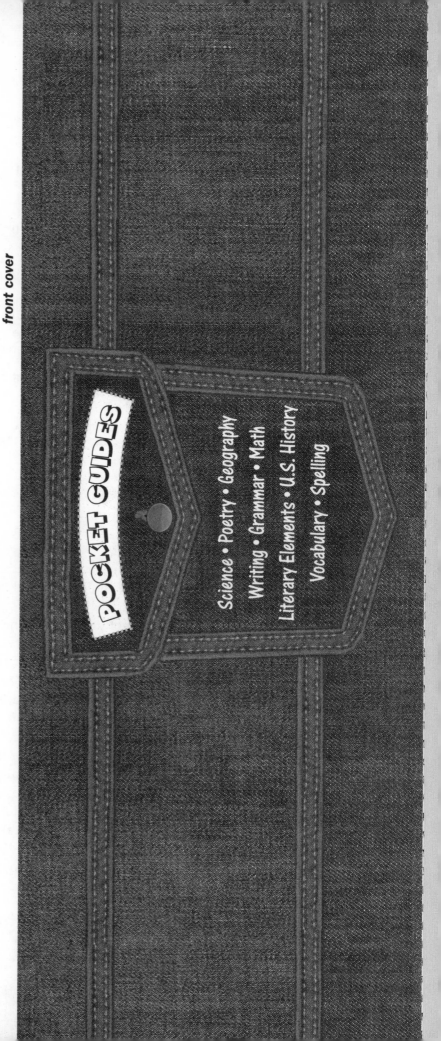

front cover

POCKET GUIDES

Science • Poetry • Geography
Writing • Grammar • Math
Literary Elements • U.S. History
Vocabulary • Spelling

8

POCKET GUIDES FOR
Language Arts

POCKET GUIDE TO
Literary Elements

POCKET GUIDE TO
Spelling

POCKET GUIDE TO
Vocabulary

POCKET GUIDE TO
Writing

POCKET GUIDE TO
Grammar

POCKET GUIDE TO
Poetry

BE A WRITING STAR!

GRAMMAR MATTERS

How do I love poetry? Let me count the ways!

Name:

Vast lurch vile squawked

My Own Spelling List

Write words here that you have trouble spelling. Refer to the list when you need to check a word's spelling.

_____

_____

_____

_____

_____

_____

_____

_____

_____

_____

_____

_____

_____

16

POCKET GUIDE TO
Spelling

SPELLING RULES!

Name: _____

Nifty Mnemonics

Mnemonics are tricks you can use to help you remember information. These nifty mnemonics will help you remember the spellings of these words.

sep**arate**	There's **a rat** in separate.
fri**end**	A friend is with you to the **end**.
v**isit**	Who **is it** that will visit?
because	**B**ig **e**lephants **c**an **a**lways **u**se **s**mall **e**lephants.
de**ss**ert	Dessert can be **so sweet**.
attendance	at ten dance •••••➤
bel**ie**ve	There's a **lie** in believe.
piece	There's **pie** in every piece.

Homophone Mnemonics

capital	city where the government has offices
capitol	building where the legislatures meet

Remember! A capitol building often has a dome.

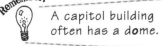

14

Table of Contents

Tricky Homophones 4

Commonly Misspelled Words 6

Possessives & Contractions 8

Spelling Rules 10

Nifty Mnemonics 14

My Own Spelling List 16

3

| meet | come together |
| meat | edible part of an animal |

Remember! You **eat** m**eat**.

| principle | a guideline |
| principal | a person who is the head of a school |

Remember! Your princi**pal** is your **pal**.

| stationary | not moving |
| stationery | pap**er** you write lett**er**s on |

Remember! Write your lett**er** on some station**ery**.

| affect | a verb that means influence |
| effect | the result |

Remember!

RAVEN: Remember:
Affect
Verb
Effect
Noun

15

Tricky Homophones

Homophones are words that sound alike but are spelled differently. For each homophone on this list, you'll find a sentence that shows how to use it correctly.

1. to — I went **to** the store
   two — Sam is **two** years old.
   too — Is Ana here, **too**?

2. threw — Norma **threw** the ball
   through — Isaac ran **through** the park

3. their — The kids played in **their** yard.
   there — The cat always sleeps **there**.
   they're — **They're** our neighbors.

4. passed — Jen **passed** the test.
   past — History is the story of the **past**.

5. scene — The first **scene** of the play was the best.
   seen — The boy did not want to be **seen**.

6. wear — Be sure the **wear** a warm coat.
   where — **Where** did the puppy go?

7. cent — I refuse to spend one **cent**!
   sent — Allan **sent** his mother a card.
   scent — The **scent** of the flowers was overwhelming.

8. know — We **know** about the party.
   no — Alex said **no** to the offer.

4

---

2. **A syllable break often occurs where a prefix or suffix has been added to a root word.**

un do   dis cour age   grace ful

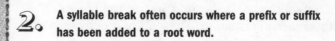

3. **When you need to break up a word because you don't have enough space at the end of a line, you can only do so between syllables.**

*Audrey quickly discovered that if she rode her **bi-cycle** to school, she was rarely late.*

4. **Never break up a one-syllable word with a hyphen.**

13

Syllabication Rules

Why do you need to know how to break words into syllables? It will help you spell words—especially long words, and it will help you use hyphenation correctly.

A syllable is a unit of sound with one vowel sound. For example, *spel ling* has two vowel sounds and, therefore, two syllables.

Here are some rules to help you break words into syllables.

1. **A syllable break often occurs between double letters.**

bit ter   hap py   let ter

12

---

9. hear — They did not **hear** the bell ring.
   here — The game will be **here**.
10. pair — Nelson needs a **pair** of skates.
    pear — The **pear** tree is full of fruit.
11. roll — The dog ate the girl's **roll**.
    role — Malika has a **role** in the play.
12. hole — The roof leaked because of the **hole**.
    whole — June ate the **whole** sandwich.
13. break — Don't **break** the glass!
    brake — The bicycle's **brake** is on.
14. your — Danny took **your** umbrella.
    you're — **You're** going to miss the bus.
15. who's — **Who's** coming to dinner?
    whose — **Whose** job is it to rake?
16. plane — The **plane** soared overhead.
    plain — She wore a **plain** dress.
17. piece — The child asked for a **piece** of pie.
    peace — The dove is a sign of **peace**.
18. its — The hamster ate all **its** food.
    it's — **It's** raining outside.
19. hour — We leave in one **hour**.
    our — **Our** teacher is new.
20. one — **One** more apple is needed.
    won — The team **won** the game.

5

Spelling Rules

All About Final E

If a word ends with a consonant and a silent *e*, drop the final *e* before you add an ending that begins with a vowel.

> *hope + ed = hoped*
> *hope + ing = hoping*

If a word ends with a consonant and a silent *e*, don't drop the final *e* before you add an ending that begins with a consonant.

> *nice + ly = nicely*
> *grace + fully = gracefully*

Final Y

Some verbs end in *y*. Change the *y* to *i* before you add *-ed*. Don't change the spelling when you add *-ing*.

> *hurry + ed = hurried*
> *hurry + ing = hurrying*

10

---

months
myself
neighbor
nickel
ocean
passed
picnic
piece
probably
quiet
really

remember	straight	tries
scared	suddenly	trouble
scary	surprise	ugly
screamed	surprised	until
shook	swung	upstairs
similar	their	visit
since	threw	wear
sitting	through	Wednesday
somebody	tomorrow	where
stood	toward	which

7

Commonly Misspelled Words

afraid	busy	forever
again	buy	friend
already	bye	grabbed
always	calendar	guess
angry	careful	happily
animals	caught	hear
another	climb	heard
anymore	clothes	herself
anyone	crowd	himself
anything	decided	hitting
anyway	different	hungry
awhile	enough	instead
beautiful	everybody	knew
before	everyone	knows
believe	everything	laugh
bottom	everywhere	laughed
bought	favorite	lightning
break	feel	listen
breakfast	February	minute
brought	finish	minutes

Double or Not?
If a word ends with one consonant that follows a short vowel sound, double the final consonant before you add an ending that begins with a vowel.

> hop + ing = hopping
> hop + ed = hopped
> run + ing = running
> run + er = runner

Don't double the final consonant when you add an ending that begins with a consonant.

> sad + ly = sadly

I Before E Rule
This rule works most of the time.

I before *e*, except after *c* or when sounding like *a*, as in *neighbor* or *weigh*.

A few exceptions are *either*, *height*, *their*, and *weird*.

Possessives & Contractions

Possessives
It's important to remember when and how to use apostrophes to make possessives.

ASK YOURSELF
Am I trying to tell about more than one thing or show ownership?

The girls coat was lost during the bus ride.

Only one girl lost her coat, so add an apostrophe and then an -s after girl.

◀ *The girl's coat was lost during the bus ride.*

Now, what if you're talking about more than one girl? To show possession with a plural noun, first add an -s, and then the apostrophe.

The girls' coats were lost during the bus ride. ▶

To form the possessive of a plural noun that does not end in an s, add an apostrophe and an -s.

The children's coats were lost during the bus ride.

Contractions
In a contraction, an apostrophe is placed where letters have been omitted. Here are some contractions.

I will	I'll
I would	I'd
I am	I'm
you will	you'll
you are	you're
let us	let's
it is	it's
they are	they're
is not	isn't
could not	couldn't
should not	shouldn't
would not	wouldn't
could have	could've
should have	should've
would have	would've
did not	didn't
do not	don't
cannot	can't
have not	haven't
was not	wasn't
she will	she'll
he will	he'll
we will	we'll
we would	we'd

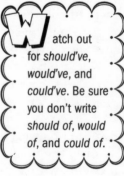

Watch out for *should've*, *would've*, and *could've*. Be sure you don't write *should of*, *would of*, and *could of*.

Could of? NO Could've!

Page 16

ot	uck	un	use	ute
bought	buck	bun	blues	cute
brought	duck	done	bruise	fruit
dot	luck	fun	chews	hoot
knot	stuck	none	clues	root
not	truck	one	lose	scoot
pot	yuck	run	news	shoot
thought		sun		suit
	ug	won	**ush**	
	bug		blush	**y**
out	dug	**unk**	brush	buy
about	hug	chunk	crush	by
doubt	mug	flunk	flush	bye
out	plug	junk	rush	cry
shout	rug	skunk		die
	tug	stunk	**ut**	dry
ow		trunk	but	eye
brow	**um**		cut	fly
cow	bum	**unny**	gut	fry
how	come	bunny	hut	hi
now	drum	funny	mutt	my
plow	dumb	honey	nut	pie
	from	sunny	shut	sigh
own	some		what	sky
cone				spy
flown				tie
known				try
moan				why
phone				
shone				

16

POCKET GUIDE TO
Poetry

How do I love poetry? Let me count the ways!

Name: _____

Page 14

ike	ime	ing	ish	ive
bike	chime	bring	dish	dive
hike	climb	king	fish	drive
like	crime	ring	wish	five
strike	dime	spring		I've
	I'm	string	**it**	live
ile	rhyme		bit	
file	time	**ink**	fit	**ize**
I'll		blink	hit	cries
isle	**in**	drink	knit	dries
mile	chin	pink	lit	eyes
smile	fin	rink	sit	flies
style	grin	sink		prize
while	pin	stink	**itch**	size
	skin	think	ditch	skies
ill	thin		itch	
chill	twin	**ip**	rich	**o**
drill	win	chip	which	blow
grill		clip		dough
hill	**ine**	dip	**its**	go
thrill	dine	drip	bits	glow
	fine	ship	hits	grow
im	mine	skip	pits	know
brim	nine	trip	quits	oh
dim	pine		wits	row
grim	shine			sew
limb				show
swim				snow
				toe

14

Table of Contents

Metaphors, Similes & Personification 4

Alliteration, Assonance & Onomatopoeia 6

Haiku and Cinquain 7

Sonnet 8

Rhyming Dictionary 10

3

I'm a poet on a quest to be the best!

ock	oke	oon	ord	ort
block	broke	goon	board	fort
clock	choke	June	bored	short
dock	joke	moon	cord	snort
knock	oak	noon	poured	sort
lock	smoke	soon	roared	sport
rock	spoke	tune	snored	
sock			sword	**ose**
talk	**old**	**oop**		blows
	bold	droop	**ore**	close
ode	cold	group	bore	clothes
code	fold	hoop	chore	flows
glowed	gold	snoop	door	knows
road	hold		floor	rose
showed	told	**op**	for	shows
toad		chop	more	those
	ole	cop	pour	
	bowl	crop	score	**oss**
og	goal	drop	snore	boss
dog	hole	hop	store	gloss
fog	role	mop	wore	loss
frog	roll	pop	your	moss
hog	whole	prop		sauce
jog		stop	**orn**	
log		top	born	
	oom		corn	
	bloom		horn	
	boom		torn	
	broom		worn	
	zoom			

Metaphors, Similes & Personification

Writers often use figurative language to make their writing more interesting. Similes, metaphors, and personification are all examples of figurative language.

Similes

A **simile** compares two unlike things by using the words *like* or *as*. Similes might not be factually true, but they help readers to see things in a vivid way.

Her teeth sparkled *like diamonds.*

His legs went *as limp as spaghetti* when he heard the news.

Here's a short poem that includes a simile:

"The Night" by Audrey Ransome

The night is like a panther
Blacker than black
Prowling the earth
Surrounding the stars.

eeze	ent	ess	ice	ide
bees	bent	dress	dice	bride
cheese	cent	less	mice	cried
keys	scent	mess	nice	glide
knees	sent	yes	rice	hide
peas	spent		slice	ride
tease	tent	**est**	spice	sighed
skis	went	best		slide
sneeze		chest	**ick**	tried
	er	dressed	brick	wide
ell	blur	quest	kick	
bell	burr	messed	lick	**ief**
cell	fur	pest	pick	beef
sell	her	west	sick	brief
spell	purr		thick	chief
yell	sir	**et**	trick	leaf
	stir	bet		thief
en	were	get	**id**	
den		yet	bid	**ight**
men	**erse**	wet	did	bite
ten	curse		grid	bright
then	nurse	**ew**	hid	fight
when	purse	blue	kid	kite
	verse	clue	slid	light
end	worse	do		might
bend		drew		night
friend	**ert**	knew		sight
send	dirt	stew		white
spend	shirt	zoo		write
	skirt			

Panel 12

aw	each	ee	eek	mean
claw	beach	bee	beak	queen
law	peach	free	cheek	seen
saw	reach	key	freak	teen
straw	teach	knee	peek	
		me	sneak	**eep**
awn	**eck**	pea	speak	cheap
dawn	check	sea	weak	deep
drawn	deck	see	week	jeep
gone	neck	she		keep
on	wreck	ski	**eel**	peep
yawn		tea	deal	sweep
	ed	tree	feel	
ay	ahead		peel	**eer**
day	bed	**eed**	real	cheer
gray	dead	bead	seal	clear
hey	fed	bleed	wheel	fear
spray	head	feed		here
they	led	greed	**eem**	rear
way	red	need	cream	smear
	said	read	scream	tear
aze	sled	seed	seem	year
blaze	spread	steed	stream	
craze	thread	weed		**eet**
days	wed		**een**	beat
maze			bean	feet
pays			clean	heat
phase			green	meat
weights			lean	street

12

Panel 5

Metaphors

Like a simile, a **metaphor** compares two things that are not alike. But in a metaphor, the words *like*, *as* or *than* are not used. A metaphor doesn't say something is **like** another thing. It says it **is** another thing.

His eyes *are piercing lasers.*

The grass *is a great green blanket, soft and perfect.*

Here's a famous poem that uses metaphor.

"Fog" by Carl Sandburg
The fog comes
On little cat feet.

It sits looking
Over harbor and city
On silent haunches
And then moves on.

Personification

Personification is a type of metaphor in which an animal, object, or idea is given human qualities.

The ocean *dared us* to dive in.

5

Panel 10

Rhyming Dictionary

This mini-rhyming dictionary lists words by the beginning vowel sound—a, e, i, o, u, and y.

ab	act	aff	ain	ake
blab	backed	calf	brain	bake
cab	fact	graph	cane	cake
crab	snacked	half	chain	lake
grab		laugh	drain	make
lab	**ad**		lane	shake
	add	**ag**	pain	snake
ace	bad	bag	rain	
base	dad	brag	train	**ale**
case	had	drag		fail
chase	mad	flag	**air**	male
face	pad		bare	nail
place	sad	**age**	bear	sail
space		cage	chair	snail
	ade	page	fair	tale
ack	aid	rage	pair	whale
back	afraid		stare	
black	grade	**aim**	tear	**all**
pack	played	became	there	ball
shack	shade	blame	where	call
smack	stayed	frame		mall
snack		game		small
		shame		tall
				wall

10

Panel 7

Haiku

Haiku is a form of poetry that began long ago in Japan. A haiku has three lines and the following syllable pattern:

Line 1	5 syllables	Blues merge with purples
Line 2	7 syllables	Iridescently glowing
Line 3	5 syllables	As the sun departs

In a haiku, the poet usually tries to capture a moment or thought about nature.

Cinquain

A cinquain is a poem with five lines and that has the following syllable pattern:

Line 1	2 syllables	Listen . . .
Line 2	4 syllables	With faint dry sound
Line 3	6 syllables	Like steps of passing ghosts
Line 4	8 syllables	The leaves, frost-crisp'd, break from trees
Line 5	2 syllables	And fall.

Phrases in a cinquain can run over from one line to the next.

7

Alliteration, Assonance & Onomatopoeia

Poetry is like music. Poets use various techniques to play with the sound, or music, of their poetry. Alliteration, assonance, and onomatopoeia—as well as rhyme—are techniques poets can use.

Alliteration

Alliteration is the repetition of the initial sound in two or more words.

Try to tame the tiger.

Assonance

Assonance is the repetition of vowel sounds.

Go slow in the snow.

Onomatopoeia

This term refers to words that imitate sounds, such as "buzz" or "ding." Here's a poem that uses onomatopoeia.

Spring Zing

Rustling . . .
  Rippling . . .
    Flutter,
      Flap;
Bubbling . . .
  Billowing . . .
    Crackle . . .
      Crack
Stirring . . .
  Whirring . . .
    Slither,
      Snap!

6

---

am	and	ar	ash	atch
clam	band	bar	cash	batch
ham	brand	car	crash	latch
jam	land	far	flash	scratch
lamb	sand	jar	smash	
slam			trash	**ate**
	ang	**ark**		bait
amp	hang	bark	**ass**	date
camp	rang	dark	brass	eight
champ	sang	shark	glass	great
damp		spark	grass	late
stamp	**ank**		mass	skate
	bank	**arm**		straight
an	crank	charm	**ast**	
ban	thank	farm	blast	**atter**
can		harm	cast	batter
fan	**ap**		last	chatter
man	cap	**art**	passed	flatter
pan	clap	heart		ladder
plan	map	mart	**at**	sadder
tan	nap	part	bat	
	rap	start	cat	**ave**
ance	snap		flat	brave
chance		**ary**	mat	cave
dance	**ape**	cherry	splat	save
France	cape	dairy	that	
pants	grape	hairy		
	scrape	merry		
	tape	very		

11

Sonnet

A sonnet is a fourteen-line poem written in iambic pentameter that follows a particular rhyme scheme. One rhyme scheme is *abab cdcd efef gg*. This is called an English or Shakespearean sonnet. The other rhyme scheme is *abba cddc cfgcfg*. This is called an Italian or Petrarchan sonnet.

Iambic Pentameter

What is iambic pentameter? This refers to the pattern of stressed and unstressed beats in a line of poetry. Here is the pattern in a line from a sonnet.

How do I love thee? Let me count the ways.

Notice that there are five pairs of stressed and unstressed beats in this line. Each pair is called and "iamb."

8

Here is a famous example of a sonnet by William Shakespeare.

Sonnet XVIII

"Shall I compare thee to a summer's day?"

Shall I compare thee to a summer's day?	a
Thou art more lovely and more temperate:	b
Rough winds do shake the darling buds of May,	a
And summer's lease hath all too short a date:	b
Sometime too hot the eye of heaven shines,	c
And often is his gold complexion dimm'd;	d
And every fair from fair sometime declines,	c
By chance, or nature's changing course, untrimm'd;	d
But thy eternal summer shall not fade,	e
Nor lose possession of that fair thou owest;	f
Nor shall Death brag thou wander'st in his shade,	e
When in eternal lines to time thou growest;	f
So long as men can breathe, or eyes can see,	g
So long lives this, and this gives life to thee.	g

9

My Favorite Stories and Books

Use this page to list some of your favorite books or stories.

Title	Author

16

POCKET GUIDE TO
Literary Elements

KNOW YOUR LITERARY ELEMENTS!

Name: _____

Flashback & Foreshadowing

> *Flashback* is an interruption in the story to tell about events from the past.

Here's an example of flashback:

> *Luisa stood next to her mother, ready to begin kneading the dough. Suddenly, the yeasty smell of dough took her back to six months before, when her grandmother had come for a visit. She, her mother, and her grandmother had been kneading bread when the phone call came. Luisa froze as she thought of this.*

> *Foreshadowing* is to suggest beforehand what is going to happen later on.

Here's an example of foreshadowing.

> *The heavy coins made his pockets sag, so Alex quickly emptied the change onto the table. He didn't need change for the bus since his mother was driving him to school.*

> *. . . later that afternoon, as the doors of the bus closed, with Alex still standing on the corner, he thought back to those heavy coins.*

14

Table of Contents

Plot 4

Character 6

Setting 8

Theme 9

Point of View 10

Figurative Language 12

Flashback & Foreshadowing 14

Graphic Organizer 15

My Favorite Stories and Books 16

3

`2`

Graphic Organizer

You can use a graphic organizer like this to help you write about the literary elements in a book or story. Copy this onto another sheet of paper and fill it in.

Setting

Characters

Title: _____

Author: _____

Plot

Theme

`15`

Plot

> *Plot* is the series of related events that make up the story.

Most plots involve resolving some kind of conflict and follow this pattern:

- The **introduction** tells who the main character or characters are and what the conflict or problem is.
- **Complications** develop as the characters struggle with different possible solutions.
- In the **climax**, the main character or characters make a final decision that settles the conflict.
- The story ends with the **resolution**: the writer suggests what the characters feel or do, now that the conflict is resolved.

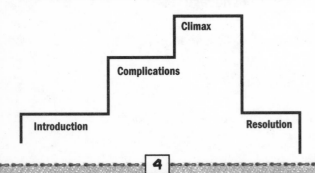

Climax

Complications

Introduction

Resolution

`4`

Personification

Personification gives human qualities to animals, objects, or ideas.

> The ocean *dared us* to dive in.

Hyperbole

Hyperbole is obvious exaggeration, which is usually funny.

> *The music was so loud, you could hear it in the next time zone.*

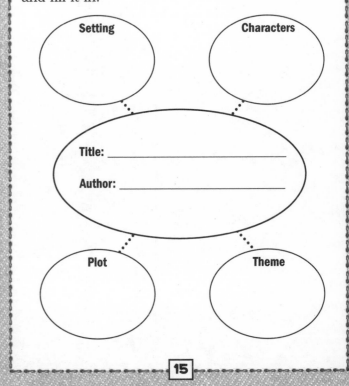

Imagery

Imagery is language that appeals to the senses.

> a *freezing*-cold snow cone
>
> the *fragile* and *gentle* touch of a butterfly's wings
>
> the *screeching* cry of an owl

Onomatopoeia

Onomatopoeia refers to words that imitate sounds, such as "buzz" or "ding."

> The leaves *crunched* and *crackled* under our footsteps.

`13`

Figurative Language

Writers often use figurative language to make their writing more interesting. Here are some examples of figurative language.

Similes

A simile compares two unlike things by using the words *like* or *as*. Similes might not be factually true, but they help readers to see things in a vivid way.

> The hurricane was *like a huge beast trying to devour us.*

> His legs were *as limp as spaghetti when he heard the news.*

Metaphors

Like a simile, a metaphor compares two things that are not alike without using the words *like, as,* or *than.* A metaphor doesn't say something is **like** another thing. It says it **is** another thing.

> His eyes *are piercing lasers.*

> The grass *is a great green blanket, soft and perfect.*

12

A conflict in a story may be internal or external.

External Conflict

The main character struggles with another person or with an outside force, such as a blizzard.

Internal Conflict

The main character struggles with opposing ideas or feelings within his or her own mind, like wanting to make friends at a new school but also being very shy.

> Should I talk to her? No. I can't. I'll just keep quiet.

5

Point of View

> The *point of view* in a literary work is the vantage point from which the story is told.

There are three points of view from which a story can be told.

First Person

The person telling the story is a character in the story, and uses *I* and *me.*

> I think . . .

10

When you think about a character, ask yourself:

What does the character say?

What does the character think?

What does the character do?

How does the character look?

What does the character feel?

7

Character

> *Character* simply means a person or other figure who is part of a story.

Characterization is how the writer reveals what a character is like. Writers do this in different ways:

Direct Characterization: The writer tells the reader what the character is like.

> *Example: "Anthony was a funny and relaxed person."*

Indirect Characterization: The writer gives the actual words of the character, tells what the character is thinking and feeling, tells about the character's actions, or tells how others respond to the character.

> *Example: "Lisa jumped up nervously when she heard the knock on door."*

Third-Person Limited

The thoughts and feelings of just one character are given. This person is referred to in the third person, e.g., he or she.

Pete felt nervous about the race.

Omniscient

The narrator tells what everyone in the story is thinking and feeling.

Sophia was wondering how long the race would last.

Pete felt nervous about the race.

Chloe was sure she'd come in first.

Setting

> *Setting* is the time and place in which story events occur.

Ask Yourself

When you think about the **setting** of a book:
When does this story take place?
Where does this story take place?
How does the setting affect the outcome of the story or book?

Theme

> *Theme* is the major idea or lesson that a story conveys about life. It's the big idea the reader takes away from the story.

Keep in mind:

1. Though there are exceptions, authors seldom state their intended theme directly.
2. It's usually up to the readers to discover the theme for themselves. Some stories may have more than one theme.
3. Different readers may find different themes in the same story.
4. Very occasionally, readers may find themes that even the authors themselves were not conscious of while writing.

Ask Yourself

When you think about theme:
What is the **big idea** in the story?
What **lesson** did the main character learn?

Page 16

	Synonyms	Antonyms
scared **adj.**	terrified, fearful	brave, bold
shy **adj.**	bashful, timid	bold, obtrusive
sick **adj.**	ailing, indisposed	healthy, strong
small **adj.**	tiny, minute	huge, enormous
smart **adj.**	intelligent, clever	dull, stupid
special **adj.**	unique, distinctive	everyday, ordinary
strange **adj.**	odd, different	normal, ordinary
strong **adj.**	powerful, mighty	weak, fragile
very **adv.**	greatly, hugely	minimally
walk **v.**	step, traipse, amble, stroll	

POCKET GUIDE TO Vocabulary

VOCAB IS FAB!

Name: _____

Page 14

	Synonyms	Antonyms
cry **v.**	sob, weep	laugh
easy **adj.**	facile, simple,	hard, difficult
fast **adj.**	quick, speedy, swift	slow, lethargic
funny **adj.**	amusing, comical, hilarious	sad, gloomy
give **v.**	contribute, grant, present	grab, seize, take
good **adj.**	excellent, fine,	bad, intolerable
great **adj.**	stupendous, superb	horrible, horrific
happy **adj.**	glad, joyful, thrilled	downcast, miserable
hard **adj.**	difficult, tough	simple, effortless
hot **adj.**	scorching, boiling, sizzling	frigid, chilly
hurt **v.**	injure, harm	benefit, aid
large **adj.**	huge, enormous, colossal	tiny, small
laugh **v.**	chuckle, snicker, giggle	cry, sob
like **v.**	prefer, admire, esteem	dislike, disdain
little **adj.**	small, tiny, petite	huge, enormous

Table of Contents

Prefixes and Suffixes 4

Latin and Greek Roots 6

Borrowed Words 8

Portmanteaus and Acronyms 9

Avoiding Overused Words 10

Mini-Thesaurus 13

2

	Synonyms	Antonyms
look **v.**	stare, ogle, gawk	ignore, overlook
loud **adj.**	blaring, piercing, roaring	soft, subdued
many **adj.**	numerous, multitudinous	few, handful
mean **adj.**	cruel, brutish	kind, gentle
new **adj.**	fresh, modern	old, dated
nice **adj.**	congenial, pleasing	mean, unpleasant
old **adj.**	dated, worn-out	fresh, modern
plain **adj.**	simple, unadorned	elaborate, ornate
pretty **adj.**	attractive, good-looking	homely, ugly
quiet **adj.**	silent, hushed	loud, blaring
really **adv.**	actually, genuinely	
right **adj.**	correct, accurate	wrong, mistaken
run **v.**	dash, scamper, scoot	dawdle, crawl
sad **adj.**	melancholy, heavy-hearted	happy, joyful
say **v.**	express, state, declare	refrain, withhold

15

Prefixes and Suffixes

Prefixes and suffixes are word parts added to the beginning or ending of a base, or root, word. If you know the meanings of important prefixes and suffixes, it can help you figure out the meaning of a word.

Prefixes

A prefix is added to the beginning of a word. It changes the meaning of the word.

dis- + approve = disapprove

Prefix	Meaning	Example
ad-	toward, to	advocate
circum-	around	circumvent
ex-	out	extract
re-	again, back	reappear, repay
un-, dis-, non-	not, the opposite of	unfair, dishonor, nonprofit
mis-, il-	wrongly, badly	misjudge, illegal
pre-	before	preview
post-	after	postdated
bi-	having two of; twice	bicycle, biannual
im-, in-	not, without, in, into	imbalance, insecure
sub-	under	submarine
inter-	between	intersection

4

Mini-Thesaurus

	Synonyms	Antonyms
angry **adj.**	enraged, furious, livid	happy, glad
answer **v.**	reply, respond, retort	ask, question
ask **v.**	question, inquire	answer, retort
bad **adj.**	horrible, lousy, terrible	wonderful, great
big **adj.**	enormous, huge, large	small, tiny
brave **adj.**	bold, courageous	scared, timid
bright **adj.**	beaming, brilliant, lustrous	dim, dull
carefully **adv.**	cautiously, safely	carelessly
cold **adj.**	freezing, chilly, frigid	warm, hot

13

Card 12

Lots	Ask	Happy
Tons	Demand	Joyful
Plenty	Entreat	Delighted
Copious	Question	Content
Myriad	Beg	Merry
Scads	Query	Ecstatic
Oodles	Inquire	Good-humored
Innumerable	Request	Upbeat
Many	Implore	Blissful

Funny

Ridiculous
Laughable
Whimsical
Rib-tickling
Hilarious
Jolly

12

Card 5

Suffixes

A suffix is added to the end of a word. It changes the word from one part of speech to another.

grace + -ful = graceful

Suffix	Meaning	Example
-ful	full of	tasteful
-able, -ible	capable or worthy of	irresistible
-ness	state, condition, or quality of	happiness
-less	without, not having	blameless
-ist	one who does or makes	artist
-ment	the act, state, quality, or result of	statement
-er, -or	something or someone that does	baker, actor
-ify	makes the word a verb	terrify
-ity	condition or state	sanity
-ious	full of	anxious
-al	relating to	natural
-ize	to cause	vocalize

art - ist   *taste - ful*

5

Card 10

Avoiding Overused Words

To spice up your writing, replace tired, overused words with more descriptive ones.

Big	Beautiful	Bad
massive	gorgeous	evil
immense	ravishing	sinister
monolithic	exquisite	wrong
stupendous	comely	wicked
whopping	attractive	vile
vast	lovely	base
king-size	resplendent	corrupt
hulking	glorious	harmful
gargantuan	picturesque	hurtful
colossal	stunning	offensive
monumental	splendid	dreadful
humongous	pulchritudinous	appalling
momentous	enchanting	repulsive
prominent	divine	disgusting
	breathtaking	atrocious
		mediocre

10

Card 7

Greek

aero = air	aerobics, aerial, aerate
belli = war	rebellion, belligerent
pan = all	panacea, pandemonium, panorama
chronos = time	chronic, chronicle, synchronize
phon = sound	megaphone, phonics, symphony
mech = machine	mechanic, mechanize
path = suffer	pathetic, sympathy, pathology
geo = earth	geography, geology, geometry
photo = light	photograph, photogenic, telephoto
auto = self	autobiography, automatic

7

Latin and Greek Roots

Many words in English contain Latin or Greek roots. Here are some common roots. Knowing them will help you figure out the meaning of new words you encounter.

Latin

aud = hear	audition, audible, audience
grat = pleasing	congratulate, gratitude, gratify
ject = throw	reject, inject, conjecture
nav = ship	navigate, naval, navigable
ped = foot	pedal, pedestal, biped
numer = number	numeral, numerous, enumerate
liber = free	liberal, liberate
clar = clear	clarity, declare, clarion
dict = say	dictate, predict, dictator
pop = people	population, populous, popular
corp = body	corporation, corporal
aqua = water	aquarium, aquamarine, aqueduct
port = carry	transport, porter, comport

6

Good	Walk	Said
benevolent	pace	bellowed
angelic	stagger	whispered
fortunate	shamble	shouted
virtuous	stomp	replied
astonishing	plod	squawked
outstanding	trample	muttered
proficient	lumber	blurted
satisfactory	march	
fantastic	clomp	**Very**
phenomenal	saunter	astonishingly
wonderful	trudge	amazingly
	parade	outstandingly
	amble	momentously
	lurch	quite
		perfectly
		utterly

11

Borrowed Words

English has borrowed many words from other cultures. Here are some examples.

Spanish
rodeo
plaza
patio
coyote
alligator
barbecue

Italian
ditto
confetti
opera
umbrella
ravioli

German
kindergarten
dollar
noodle
blitz
nickel
pretzel

Arabic
almanac
sheik
syrup
magazine

Dutch
cookie
frolic
loiter
boss
waffle

Swedish
boulder
flounder
scuffle
lug
spry
wicker

Native American
pecan
squash
moose
chipmunk

Hindi
bungalow
dinghy
bangle
cot

French
café
eclair
crayon
chauffeur
corduroy
denim
picnic

8

Portmanteaus

A portmanteau is a word that is a blend of two other words.

squall + squeak = squawk
squirm + wiggle = squiggle
flame + glare = flare
situation + comedy = sitcom
travel + monologue = travelogue
motor + hotel = motel

Acronyms

An acronym is a word made from the first letters of a phrase.

*scuba = **s**elf-**c**ontained **u**nderwater **b**reathing **a**pparatus*
*laser = **l**ight **a**mplification by **s**timulated **e**mission of **r**adiation*
*modem = **mo**dulator and **dem**odulator*
*snafu = **s**ituation **n**ow **a**ll **f**ouled **u**p*
*radar = **ra**dio **d**etection **a**nd **r**anging*

9

An Editing Checklist

❑ **1.** Is each sentence a complete sentence?

❑ **2.** Are the nouns precise and the verbs strong?

❑ **3.** Does each sentence begin with a capital letter and end with a punctuation mark?

❑ **4.** Does each paragraph have a main idea?

❑ **5.** Do all the sentences in a paragraph support the main idea?

❑ **6.** Are the sentences in each paragraph in an order that makes sense?

This paragraph makes a lot of sense!

16

POCKET GUIDE TO

Writing

BE A WRITING STAR!

Name: _____

Book Report

A book report should include a title, a theme statement, a summary of the book, and your opinion about the book.

❶ *Title:* Check with your teacher, but usually the title of the book report is the title of the book (either underlined or in all capital letters) followed by the author's name.

❷ *Theme Statement:* In the opening paragraph, be sure to include a sentence that states the book's theme, or main idea. The theme usually tells what the main character learned or tells why the author wrote the book.

❸ *Summary of the Story:* To summarize the story, tell about the plot (what happens to the main characters). Be sure you explain who the important characters are.

❹ *Your Opinion:* In a sentence or two, tell whether or not you liked the book.

14

Table of Contents

A Friendly Letter 4

A Business Letter 6

Paragraphs 8

5 Fabulous Writing Tips 12

Transition Words .13

Book Report 14

An Editing Checklist 16

3

Here's an example of a short book report.

❶ _Island of the Blue Dolphins_ by Scott O'Dell

❷ _Island of the Blue Dolphins_ tells the story of a courageous girl who learns to survive completely on her own after she's left alone on an island.

❸ The main character, Karana, is an Indian girl who is left behind as the rest of her tribe leaves the island they have always lived on. She jumps off the ship that is carrying everyone away when she realizes her little brother is still on the beach. Soon, her brother is killed by wild dogs, and she is left completely alone. She builds a shelter for herself, learns to hunt for food, and even befriends a wild dog. After many years, another ship arrives, and she is taken to a mission. There she learns that none of the people in her tribe have survived.

❹ This amazing book kept me on the edge of my seat. Karana was so brave and smart. She also loved and respected all the animals she encountered. This is an exciting book, and I recommend it to anyone who likes adventure stories.

A Friendly Letter

254 Fifth Street
Oak River, NJ 07777
December 18, 2005 **❶**

Dear Alex, **❷**

Hi! How is everything in Texas? We really miss you here in New Jersey. Is it warm there? We haven't had any snow yet, but it's been really cold.

Basketball practice has just begun. Our first game is in two weeks. We have to work extra hard now that you're gone. No one comes close to scoring as many points as you did! When is your first game? **❸**

I hope you can come visit us during spring break like we planned. Everyone is really looking forward to seeing you.

Your friend, **❹**

Chris **❺**

Transition Words

These words help signal the reader that you're moving from one idea to another.

Enumerative	Sequence	Cause & Effect
also	before	because
another	during	therefore
second	finally	thus
for example	at the start	consequently
furthermore	first	as a result of
in addition	last	
some	soon	**Compare &**
others	formerly	**Contrast**
too	next	on the other hand
likewise	then	instead
a few	someday	however
as well as	now	different from
	eventually	same as, similar to
Emphasizing	when	by contrast
mainly	whenever	unlike
most important	later	although
chief	after	
primarily	immediately	**Concluding**
especially	long ago	as a result
	since	in conclusion
	today	in summary

5 Fabulous Writing Tips

Show, Don't Tell!
Samantha *was happy* when she saw her cousin.
Better: Samantha *jumped up* and *clapped* her hands when she saw her cousin.

Add Excitement With Adjectives and Adverbs.
Malik glanced at the dog.
Better: Malik glanced *nervously* at the *snarling* dog.

Choose Just the Right Words.
Food littered the floor of the movie theater.
Better: *Popcorn and gum* littered the floor of the movie theater.

Jose *went* across the room.
Better: Jose *crept* across the room.

Vary Your Sentences.
The dog is cute. The dog is small. The dog is brown. The dog's eyes are sweet.
Better: The dog is irresistible. His sweet eyes complement his silky brown fur. Though tiny in size, he's a big bundle of fun.

Avoid the Passive Voice.
Allan was driven to school by Eva.
Better: Eva drove Allan to school

12

---

1 **Heading** — The address of the person writing the letter and the date.

2 **Greeting** — Begins with *Dear*, and includes the name of the person the letter is to. It is followed by a comma.

3 **Body** — The main part of the letter.

4 **Closing** — This starts with a capital letter and is followed by a comma.

5 **Signature** — The signed name of the letter writer.

✔ Friendly Letter Rubric

☐ **1.** Does my letter have all of these parts?
   a. heading
   b. greeting
   c. body
   d. closing
   e. signature

☐ **2.** Is my spelling, capitalization, and punctuation correct?

5

Descriptive
A **descriptive paragraph** describes something. It should have a topic sentence that tells the reader what is being described, and supporting sentences that are descriptive.

✔ Descriptive Writing Rubric

☐ **1.** Does my topic sentence tell about my topic in an interesting way?

☐ **2.** Are my details precise?

☐ **3.** Is my spelling, capitalization, and punctuation correct?

10

---

1 **Heading** — The address of the person writing the letter and the date.

2 **Inside Address** — The name and address of the person to whom you are writing the letter.

3 **Salutation** — May begin with *Dear*, and includes the name of the person the letter is to. It is followed by a colon.

4 **Body** — States the letter's purpose.

5 **Closing** — This starts with a capital letter and is followed by a comma.

6 **Signature** — The signed name of the person who wrote the letter.

✔ Business Letter Rubric

☐ **1.** Does my letter have all of these parts?
   a. heading
   b. inside address
   c. greeting
   d. body
   e. closing
   f. signature

☐ **2.** Is my spelling, capitalization, and punctuation correct?

7

A Business Letter

①

1773 Lincoln Boulevard
Santa Monica, California 90000
January 25, 2006

②

Ms. Lila Heath
Heath Toy Company
265 8th Avenue
Belson, Utah 08888

③

Dear Ms. Heath:

    I recently purchased a game from your company called Bells & Whistles. However, it is missing a few parts. The package says it contains four whistles and three bells. The game I bought has only two whistles and two bells. **④**

    Can you send me the missing bells and whistles? One of my friends has the game, and it was fun to play. I'd really like to have all the pieces so I can play it at home with my family.

    Thanks for your help in fixing this problem.

Sincerely, **⑤**

Jason Fuentes **⑥**

6

Paragraphs

A paragraph should have a topic sentence, supporting detail sentences, and a clincher, or concluding sentence.

Here is an example of a paragraph:

Topic Sentence

A platypus is a very unique animal. It is one of the few mammals in the world that lays eggs. This furry animal has webbed feet and a duck-like bill. A male platypus has poisonous spurs on its feet. These one-of-a kind creatures are found only in Australia.

Supporting Detail Sentences

Clincher

Expository

There are different kinds of paragraphs. The paragraph about the platypus is called an **expository paragraph**. An expository paragraph tells about something or gives instructions for doing something.

8

Persuasive

In a **persuasive paragraph**, the writer tries to persuade someone to do or think something. The writer needs to include logical reasons that the reader should agree with him or her.

✔ Persuasive Writing Rubric

☐ **1.** Does my topic sentence state my opinion?

☐ **2.** Are my supporting reasons logical and sensible?

☐ **3.** Does my conclusion summarize my opinion and reasons?

☐ **4.** Is my spelling, capitalization, and punctuation correct?

11

Narrative

A **narrative paragraph** tells a story. Like all paragraphs, it should have a topic sentence. It should have a beginning, a middle, and an end.

✔ Narrative Paragraph Rubric

☐ **1.** Is my topic sentence interesting?

☐ **2.** Does my story have a beginning, middle, and an end?

☐ **3.** Have I used descriptive adjectives, specific nouns, and strong verbs?

☐ **4.** Is my spelling, capitalization, and punctuation correct?

9

Proofreading Marks

Symbol	Meaning	Example
≡ (cap)	capitalize	they visited the Grand Canyon. (cap) ≡
/	use a lowercase letter	Brianna was late for the Party.
◯ sp	spelling mistake	January is the first (motnh) of the year. sp
⊙	add a period	Manuel plays hockey ⊙
ℐ	delete	Nick is in the the seventh grade.
∧	add a word or letter	The red is missing a weel. car h
⌃,	add a comma	He ate a banana an apple, and a pear.
∿	reverse words or letters	A whale is a mammal seal. (tr)
∨	add an apostrophe	Angels father is an engineer.
❝ ❞	add quotation marks	You're late, yelled the bus driver.
#	make a space	Amelia plays theguitar.
⌒	close a space	The butter fly landed on the flower.
¶	begin a new paragraph	... to see. Finally, I feel ...

16

POCKET GUIDE TO
Grammar

GRAMMAR MATTERS

Name: _____

3

Commas

Between the day and year in a date	March 27, 1995
Between the name of a city and a state	Boise, Idaho
After the greeting and closing of a letter	Dear Arne, Yours truly,
Between a series of words in a sentence	apples, pumpkins, and squash
Before the word that joins a compound sentence	Zane walked to the corner, and then he turned into the parking lot.
To separate a noun after a direct address	Luz, please have some cake.
Before quotation marks or inside the end quotation mark	The man said, "You should be wearing a hat." "You should be wearing a hat," the man said.

14

Table of Contents

Nouns & Pronouns 4

Verbs 6

Adjectives 7

Adverbs 8

Prepositions 9

Conjunctions & Interjections 10

Sentences 11

Capitalization 12

Punctuation 13

Proofreading Marks 16

3

Use quotation marks

Around the exact words someone used when speaking	The teacher said, "Let's learn a song."
Around titles of stories	"Cinderella"
Around titles of poems	"The Midnight Ride of Paul Revere"
Around titles of songs	"Row, Row, Row Your Boat"

Use apostrophes

To form the possessive of a noun	Belinda lost the boy's book.
In contractions	She wasn't sure what to do.

Remember!

Periods are placed inside end quotation marks.

Nina said, "Let's go."

My favorite story is "Cinderella."

Nouns & Pronouns

Nouns

A **common noun** is a word that names a person, place, or thing. Nouns can also name feelings and ideas.

The *boy* skated down the *street*.

A **proper noun** names a particular person, place, or thing.

Jason skated down *Main Street*.

Nouns may be singular or plural. A **singular noun** names just one person, place, or thing.

The *rocket* blasted into space.

A **plural noun** names more than one person, place, or thing. Plurals of most nouns are formed by adding *-s* or *-es*.

The *rockets* blasted into space.
The *lunches* are ready.

Punctuation

Use Periods

At the end of declarative and imperative sentences	Today, I will visit grandma.
After most abbreviations	Dr. New York, N.Y.

Use Exclamation Marks

After exclamatory sentences	Watch out for that bat!

Use Question Marks

After interrogative sentences	What time is it?

Capitalization

Capitalize	
The pronoun I	Today, I will finish my homework.
Names of cities, states, countries and continents	Chicago, Illinois; North America
Names, initials, and titles used with names	Dr. Joan Smith
Proper adjectives	French fries
Names of lakes, rivers, and mountains	Lake Erie; Platt River; Rocky Mountains
Names of streets and street abbreviations	Main Street; Lincoln Ave.
Days, months, and holidays	Saturday; November; Thanksgiving
First, last and all important words in a movie, book, story, play, and TV show title	*Out of the Dust*; *Lord of the Rings*
The first word in a sentence	She ran in the marathon.
The first word inside a quotation mark	Luke said, "Come to my house."
Both letters in the US postal abbreviations	NY

12

Pronouns

A **pronoun** is a word that can take the place of a noun.

Ella glanced at the *puppy*. *She* glanced at *it*.

A **subject pronoun** can take the place of a noun that is the subject of a sentence.

Mr. Barnes won the marathon. *He* won the *marathon*.

An **object pronoun** can take the place of a noun that is the object of a verb or that follows a preposition.

Malik gave the *letter to Paul*.
Malik gave *it* to *him*.

Possessive Pronouns
A **possessive pronoun** shows who or what owns something.

The guitar is *mine*.

5

Conjunctions

Conjunctions are words that can join words or groups of words. *And*, *but*, and *or* are conjunctions.

Alan learned about alligators, crocodiles, *and* caimans.

Would you like vanilla *or* chocolate ice cream?

Jessica went to the store, *but* she forgot to buy milk.

Interjections

An **interjection** is a word or group of words that expresses a strong feeling.

Wow! Let's go see the fireworks.

Oh! You surprised me.

Look out! There's a bee.

10

Adjectives

An **adjective** is a word that tells more about a noun. Adjectives may describe number, color, or size. Adjectives may describe how something looks or sounds, or how something tastes, feels, or smells.

The *delicious* pie sold out quickly.

Demonstrative Adjectives
This, *that*, *these*, and *those* are **demonstrative adjectives**. They tell which one or which ones.

Those shoes will be perfect for the dance.

Comparative and Superlative Adjectives
Comparative adjectives compare two nouns or pronouns.

bigger cars   *better* tests

Superlative adjectives compare more than two nouns or pronouns.

biggest car of all   *best* test ever

7

Verbs

An **action verb** tells about the action of the subject of a sentence.

The plane *landed* safely.

A **linking verb** links the subject of a sentence to a noun or an adjective in the predicate.

The boat *was* bright blue.

Common linking verbs are *am, is, are, was, were, been,* and *seem(s)*.

Tenses

Verbs have tenses.
Present-tense verbs tell about actions that are happening now or happen regularly.

The horse *gallops* through the field.

Past-tense verbs describe actions that happened in the past.

The crowd *shouted* at the football players.

Future-tense verbs show something is going to happen.

Jordan *will try out* for the team.

6

Sentences

A **sentence** is a group of words that expresses a complete thought.

The dog jumped over the fence.

Types of Sentences

A **declarative sentence** makes a statement and ends with a period.

The island was deserted.

An **interrogative sentence** asks a question and ends with a question mark.

Who wrote the letter?

An **imperative sentence** tells someone to do something and ends with a period.

Stop listening to that music.

An **exclamatory sentence** expresses excitement and ends with an exclamation mark.

Watch out for that tree!

11

Adverbs

An **adverb** is a word that tells more about the verb. An adverb can tell how, when, or where.

Caleb jumped *quickly*.	(how)
Caleb jumped *last*.	(when)
Caleb jumped *far*.	(where)

Many adverbs end in *-ly*.

Don't use an adjective when you should use an adverb.

The dog barked loudly.
Not: The dog barked loud.

WOOF!

8

Prepositions

A **preposition** is a word that relates a noun or pronoun to another word in a sentence.

Jose works *at* the ice cream store.

Common Prepositions		
about	beside	off
above	between	on
across	by	out
after	down	outside
against	during	over
along	for	through
among	from	to
around	in	under
at	inside	until
before	into	up
behind	near	with
below	of	without

I would be **at** a loss **without** prepositions!

9

POCKET GUIDES FOR
Social Studies

POCKET GUIDE TO
Geography

BE ON TOP OF THE WORLD!

Name:

POCKET GUIDE TO
U.S. History

Have a Blast with the Past!

Name:

Fast Facts

Largest state in the United States is Alaska.

State with largest population is California.

State with smallest population is Wyoming.

Smallest state is Rhode Island.

Most populous city in the U.S. is New York City.

Highest point in the U.S. is Mt. McKinley in Alaska.

Lowest point is Death Valley in California.

Lake Baikal is the world's deepest lake. You could sink five Empire State buildings in it, one on top of the other.

The oldest capital city in the world is Damascus, Syria. It was founded about 5,000 years ago.

The lowest point on Earth is on the Dead Sea in Israel.

Mount Everest, on the Nepal-Tibet border, is the highest mountain in the world.

China has the largest population of any country in the world. About 1.1 billion people live there.

The Sahara Desert is the largest desert in the world.

Lake Superior is the largest freshwater lake in the world.

Angel Falls in Venezuela is the highest waterfall in the world.

The Andes is the longest mountain chain in the world.

Australia is the smallest continent and the largest island in the world.

The longest river in the world is the Nile River.

The river with the most volume is the Amazon River.

The world's largest lake is the salty Caspian Sea.

Mumbai (Bombay), India, is the world's most populous city (12.4 million).

16

POCKET GUIDE TO
Geography

BE ON TOP OF THE WORLD!

Name: _____

Asia

ARCTIC OCEAN

Kara Sea Laptev Sea East Siberian Sea

Barents Sea

RUSSIA

Moscow

Sea of Okhotsk

Caspian Sea KAZAKHSTAN Astana

MONGOLIA Ulaanbaatar

Black Sea Tbilisi UZBEKISTAN Tashkent KYRGYZSTAN Bishkek
Ankara Yerevan Baku TAJIKISTAN Dushanbe Beijing NORTH KOREA Pyongyang Japan Sea of Japan
ARMENIA AZERBAIJAN TURKMENISTAN Ashgabat SOUTH KOREA Seoul JAPAN
TURKEY CYPRUS SYRIA Baghdad Teheran Kabul Islamabad CHINA Yellow Sea Tokyo
LEBANON ISRAEL IRAQ IRAN AFGHANISTAN New Delhi NEPAL BHUTAN Thimphu East China Sea
JORDAN KUWAIT PAKISTAN Kathmandu PACIFIC OCEAN
BAHRAIN Riyadh QATAR BANGLADESH Dhaka Taipei
SAUDI ARABIA U.A.E. Muscat INDIA MYANMAR (BURMA) Hanoi TAIWAN
OMAN Arabian Sea LAOS Vientiane
YEMEN Bay of Bengal Yangon (Rangoon) THAILAND VIETNAM South China Sea Philippine Sea
Sanaa Bangkok CAMBODIA Manila
Red Sea INDIAN OCEAN SRI LANKA Andaman Sea Phnom Penh PHILIPPINES
Colombo Male MALDIVES Kuala Lumpur MALAYSIA BRUNEI Bandar Seri Begawan Sulu Sea
SINGAPORE Celebes Sea
Java Sea Banda Sea
Jakarta
Arafura Sea

N

0   600   1200 mi
0   600   1200 km

14

Table of Contents

Dictionary of Geographic Terms 4

United States 6

States & Capitals 8

North America 10

South America 11

Europe 12

Africa 13

Asia 14

Australia & Oceania 15

Fast Facts 16

3

Australia and Oceania

0   500   1000   1500 mi
0   500   1000   1500 km

Dictionary of Geographic Terms

archipelago: A large group or chain of islands.

basin: An area of low-lying land surrounded by higher land.

bay: Part of an ocean, sea, or lake, that extends into the land. A bay is usually smaller than a gulf.

butte: A small, flat-topped hill. A butte is smaller than a plateau or a mesa.

canyon: A deep, narrow valley with steep sides.

cape: A projecting part of a coastline that extends into an ocean, sea, gulf, bay, or lake.

gulf: Part of an ocean or sea that extends into the land. A gulf is usually larger than a bay.

island: A body of land completely surrounded by water.

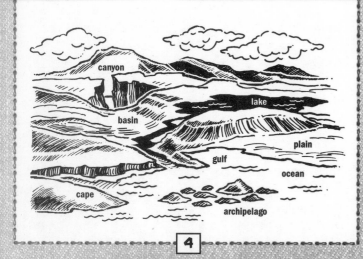

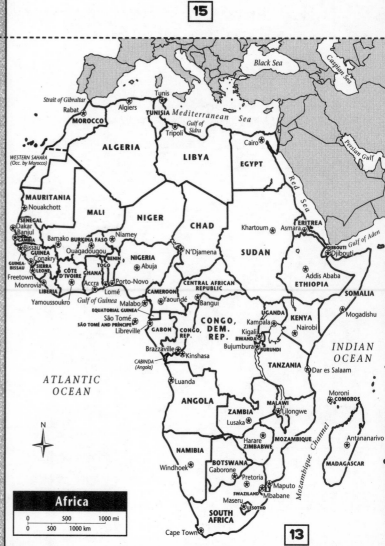

Africa

0   500   1000 mi
0   500   1000 km

Glossary (panel 5)

lake: A body of water completely surrounded by land.

mesa: A high, flat landform rising steeply above the surrounding land. A mesa is smaller than a plateau and larger than a butte.

mountain: A high, rounded or pointed landform with steep sides, higher than a hill.

mouth: The place where a river empties into another body of water.

ocean: One of the earth's four largest bodies of water.

peninsula: A body of land nearly surrounded by water.

plain: A large area of flat or nearly flat land.

plateau: A high, flat landform that rises steeply above the surrounding land. A plateau is larger than a mesa and a butte.

river: A large stream of water that flows across the land and usually empties into a lake, ocean, or other river.

strait: A narrow channel connecting two larger bodies of water.

valley: An area of low land between hills or mountains.

volcano: An opening in the earth through which lava, rock, gases, and ash are forced out.

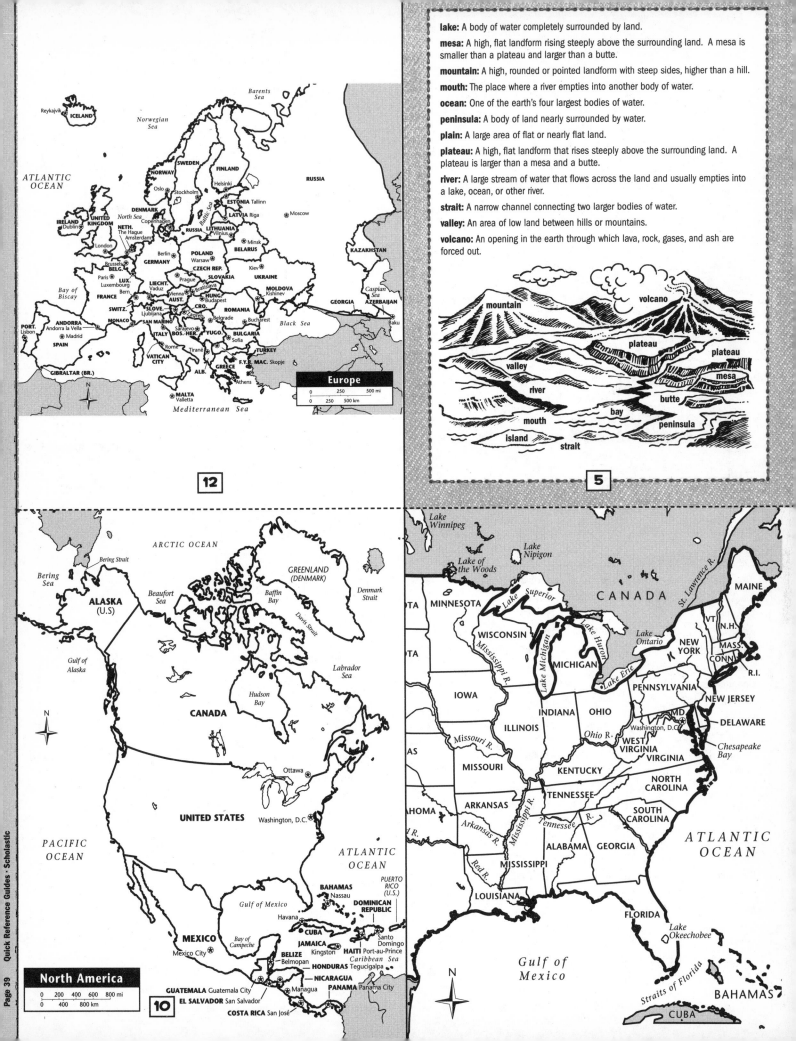

United States

WASHINGTON
OREGON
Columbia R.
Columbia R.
Snake R.
Missouri R.
MONTANA
IDAHO
WYOMING
NORTH DAK
SOUTH DAK
NEBRASKA
Platte R.
NEVADA
Great Salt Lake
UTAH
Colorado R.
COLORADO
KAN
Arkansas R.
CALIFORNIA
Colorado R.
ARIZONA
NEW MEXICO
OKL
R
TEXAS
Rio Grande
MEXICO
PACIFIC OCEAN
Lake Winnipegosis
Lake Manitoba
Saskat

United States

| 0 | 250 | 500 mi |
| 0 | 250 | 500 km |

6

South America

ATLANTIC OCEAN
Caracas
VENEZUELA
Georgetown
GUYANA
Paramaribo
SURINAME
Cayenne
FRENCH GUIANA (Fr.)
Bogotá
COLOMBIA
Quito
ECUADOR
PERU
Lima
BRAZIL
PACIFIC OCEAN
La Paz
BOLIVIA
Sucre
Brasília
PARAGUAY
Asunción
ARGENTINA
URUGUAY
Santiago
Buenos Aires
Montevideo
CHILE
San Matías Gulf
Gulf of San Jorge
Bahía Grande
Strait of Magellan
ATLANTIC OCEAN
N

South America

| 0 | 250 | 500 | 750 mi |
| 0 | 250 | 500 | 750 | 1000 km |

11

States & Capitals

Alabama	AL	Montgomery
Alaska	AK	Juneau
Arizona	AZ	Phoenix
Arkansas	AR	Little Rock
California	CA	Sacramento
Colorado	CO	Denver
Connecticut	CT	Hartford
Delaware	DE	Dover
Florida	FL	Tallahassee
Georgia	GA	Atlanta
Hawaii	HI	Honolulu
Idaho	ID	Boise
Illinois	IL	Springfield
Indiana	IN	Indianapolis
Iowa	IA	Des Moines
Kansas	KS	Topeka
Kentucky	KY	Frankfort
Louisiana	LA	Baton Rouge
Maine	ME	Augusta
Maryland	MD	Annapolis
Massachusetts	MA	Boston
Michigan	MI	Lansing
Minnesota	MN	St. Paul
Mississippi	MI	Jackson

8

Missouri	MO	Jefferson City
Montana	MT	Helena
Nebraska	NE	Lincoln
Nevada	NV	Carson City
New Hampshire	NH	Concord
New Jersey	NJ	Trenton
New Mexico	NM	Santa Fe
New York	NY	Albany
North Carolina	NC	Raleigh
North Dakota	ND	Bismarck
Ohio	OH	Columbus
Oklahoma	OK	Oklahoma City
Oregon	OR	Salem
Pennsylvania	PA	Harrisburg
Rhode Island	RI	Providence
South Carolina	SC	Columbia
South Dakota	SD	Pierre
Tennessee	TN	Nashville
Texas	TX	Austin
Utah	UT	Salt Lake City
Vermont	VT	Montpelier
Virginia	VA	Richmond
Washington	WA	Olympia
West Virginia	WV	Charleston
Wisconsin	WI	Madison
Wyoming	WY	Cheyenne

9

Quick Reference Guides · Scholastic

Our Government

The United States government has a system of checks and balances designed to prevent any branch of the government from becoming too powerful.

- can override president's veto
- can reject president's appointments
- can charge the president with wrongdoing

Legislative Branch
CONGRESS
- writes laws
- approves treaties
- passes taxes
- declares war

- can charge Supreme Court justices with wrongdoing
- can reject appointments of justices

- can veto laws passed by Congress

- can rule whether laws passed by Congress are constitutional

Executive Branch
PRESIDENT
- oversees the government
- commander-in-chief of the armed forces
- appoints government leaders
- makes treaties

- can rule whether president's actions are constitutional

- grants pardons
- appoints Supreme Court justices

Judicial Branch
SUPREME COURT AND OTHER FEDERAL COURTS
- explains the meaning of laws and treaties

16

POCKET GUIDE TO
U.S. History

Have a Blast with the Past!

Name: _____

1800–1900

1803 Louisiana Purchase doubles the size of the U.S.
1812 The U.S. fights another war with Great Britain.
1830 First wagon train crosses the Rocky Mountains.

1848 At the Seneca Falls convention, women declare their rights.
1849 The Gold Rush brings thousands to California.
1861 Civil War begins.
1865 Civil War ends.
1869 Transcontinental railroad links east and west.

14

Table of Contents

U.S. Presidents 4

Famous People in America's History 6

Important Documents 10

Famous Quotations 11

American History Time Line 12

Our Government 16

3

1900–2000

1917 U.S. enters World War I.

1929 The stock market crashes, beginning the Great Depression.

1941 Japan bombs Pearl Harbor and the U.S. enters World War II.

1945 World War II ends.

1950 Korean War begins.

1954 Supreme Court outlaws segregated schools.

1963 Civil rights protestors march in Washington, D.C.

1965 American involvement in Vietnam increases.

1989 The Berlin Wall comes down, signaling the end of the Cold War.

1991 Persian Gulf War begins and ends.

2000

2001 A terrorist attack destroys the World Trade Center in New York City.

2003 U.S./Iraq War begins.

U.S. Presidents

1	George Washington	1789-1797 ▶
2	John Adams	1797-1801
3	Thomas Jefferson	1801-1809
4	James Madison	1809-1817
5	James Monroe	1817-1825
6	John Quincy Adams	1825-1829
7	Andrew Jackson	1829-1837 ▶
8	Martin Van Buren	1837-1841
9	William H. Harrison	1841
10	John Tyler	1841-1845
11	James K. Polk	1845-1849
12	Zachary Taylor	1849-1850
13	Milliard Fillmore	1850-1853
14	Franklin Pierce	1853-1857
15	James Buchanan	1857-1861
16	Abraham Lincoln	1861-1865 ▶
17	Andrew Johnson	1865-1869
18	Ulysses S. Grant	1869-1877 ▶
19	Rutherford B. Hayes	1877-1881
20	James A. Garfield	1881
21	Chester A. Arthur	1881-1885

1600–1700

1607 English colonists settle Jamestown in Virginia.

1610 Spain establishes a colony at present-day Santa Fe in New Mexico.

1619 20 Africans are brought to Jamestown, where they become indentured servants.

1620 The Pilgrims settle New Plymouth in Massachusetts.

1700–1800

1718 French settlers found New Orleans.

1732 Georgia, the last of the 13 English colonies, is settled.

1754 Seven Years' War, or French and Indian War, begins.

1775 Battles of Lexington and Concord begin the Revolutionary War.

1776 The Declaration of Independence is adopted.

1783 Revolutionary War ends.

1787 Constitution is written.

American History Time Line

1500–1600

1500 Arrival of Europeans will forever change the lives of the millions of Native Americans living in the Americas.

1502 The first Africans arrive in the Americas.

1508 Juan Ponce de León explores Puerto Rico.

1513 Ponce de León claims Florida for Spain.

1524 Giovanni da Verrazano explores the Atlantic coast of North America.

1541 Francisco Coronado's expedition travels into what is now the Midwest.

1565 Spain establishes a permanent settlement at St. Augustine in Florida.

1585 More than 100 English settlers set up a colony at Roanoke in Virginia.

12

22	Grover Cleveland	1885–1889
23	Benjamin Harrison	1889–1893
24	Grover Cleveland	1893–1897
25	William McKinley	1897–1901
26	Theodore Roosevelt	1901–1909 ▶
27	William Howard Taft	1909–1913
28	Woodrow Wilson	1913–1921
29	Warren G. Harding	1921–1923
30	Calvin Coolidge	1923–1929
31	Herbert Hoover	1929–1933
32	Franklin D. Roosevelt	1933–1945 ▶
33	Harry S. Truman	1945–1953
34	Dwight D. Eisenhower	1953–1961
35	John F. Kennedy	1961–1963 ▶
36	Lyndon B. Johnson	1963–1969
37	Richard M. Nixon	1969–1974
38	Gerald R. Ford	1974–1977
39	Jimmy Carter	1977–1981
40	Ronald Reagan	1981–1989
41	George Bush	1989–1993
42	Bill Clinton	1993–2001
43	George W. Bush	2001– ▶

5

Important Documents

Mayflower Compact A 1620 agreement in which the Pilgrims decided to set up a government and make fair laws for their settlement at Plymouth.

Declaration of Independence This official document was issued by the Second Continental Congress in 1776. Its goal was to explain to the world why the American colonies should break away from Great Britain. Thomas Jefferson wrote most of the document.

Constitution The plan of government for the United States, outlined during the Constitutional Convention in 1787.

Bill of Rights The first ten amendments, or additions, to the constitution, which were added in 1791. They are called the Bill of Rights because they list the most important rights and freedoms of Americans. These rights include freedom of speech, religion, and the press, and the right to a fair trial.

Emancipation Proclamation President Lincoln issued this official announcement proclaiming the freedom of slaves in the Confederacy in 1862.

10

Hernando Cortés (1485–1547)
Spanish conquistador who defeated the Aztecs and founded Mexico City.

Jefferson Davis (1808–1889)
President of the Confederate States during the Civil War.

Deganawida (1500s)
A founder of the Iroquois Confederacy.

Frederick Douglass (1817–1895)
Abolitionist and writer who told about his own enslavement.

Leif Ericson (980?–1025?)
Viking explorer who was probably the first European to explore North America.

Benjamin Franklin (1706–1790)
Scientist, writer, signer of the Declaration of Independence, and delegate to the Constitutional Convention.

Ulysses S. Grant (1822–1885)
18th President of the United States and Commander of the Union Army from 1864 to 1865.

7

Famous People in America's History

Crispus Attucks (1723?–1770)
Former slave and patriot who was the first person killed in the Boston Massacre.

Benjamin Banneker (1731–1806)
Helped plan Washington, D.C.

Jacques Cartier (1491–1557)
French explorer who was the first European to sail the St. Lawrence River.

William Clark (1770–1838)
Explorer of the Louisiana Purchase.

Christopher Columbus (1451?–1506)
Italian explorer who was sent by Queen Isabella of Spain on a voyage to the "New World."

6

Famous Quotations

..but as for me, give me liberty or give me death!

Patrick Henry, speech, 1775

. . . I could work as much and eat as much as a man—when I could get it—and bear the lash as well? And ain't I a woman?

. . .ask not what your country can do for you; ask what you can do for your country.

Sojourner Truth, speech at a women's rights convention in 1851

The only thing we have to fear is fear itself.

John F. Kennedy, Inaugural Address, 1961

I have a dream that my four little children will one day live in a nation where they will not be judged by the color of their skin but by the content of their character.

Franklin D. Roosevelt, First Inaugural Address, 1933

Martin Luther King, Jr., speech, 1963

11

Famous People in America's History

Anne Hutchinson (1591–1643)
Puritan who founded Portsmouth, Rhode Island.

Martin Luther King, Jr. (1929–1968)
Civil rights leader during the 1950s and 1960s.

Chief Joseph (1840–1904)
Nez Perce leader

Meriwether Lewis (1774–1809)
Explorer of the Louisiana Purchase.

Thurgood Marshall (1907–1993)
Civil rights lawyer who became the first African–American Supreme Court Justice.

Sandra Day O'Connor (1930 –)
First woman to become a Supreme Court Justice.

8

Rosa Parks (1913–)
Civil rights leader who fought segregation by protesting on city buses in Montgomery, Alabama.

Juan Ponce de León (1460?–1521)
Spanish explorer who searched in Florida for the fountain of youth.

Sacajawea (1787?–1812)
Shoshone guide and translator for the Lewis and Clark expedition.

Junipero Serra (1713–1784)
Roman Catholic missionary who built missions in California.

Squanto (1585?–1622)
Pawtuxet Native American who helped the Pilgrims at Plymouth.

Harriet Tubman (1820?–1913)
Abolitionist and Underground Railroad conductor.

9

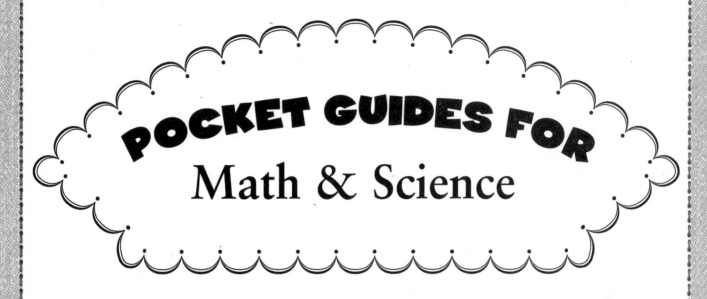

POCKET GUIDES FOR
Math & Science

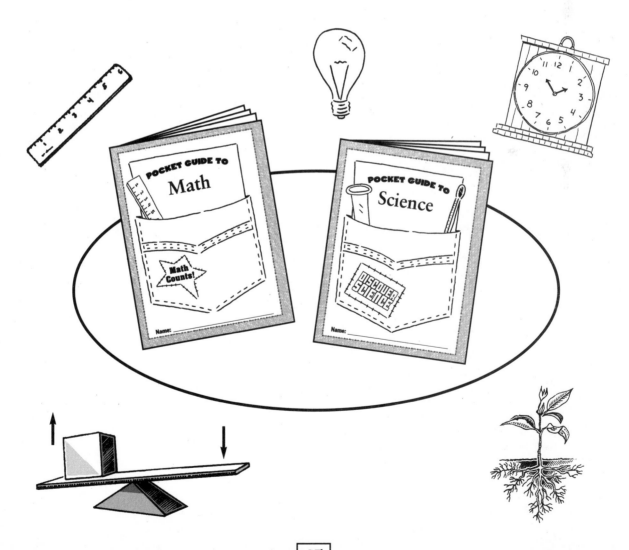

POCKET GUIDE TO
Math

Math Counts!

Name:

POCKET GUIDE TO
Science

DISCOVER SCIENCE

Name:

Mental Math Tips

1) Make easy numbers.

Some numbers are easier to work with. For example, you can probably do these math problems quickly.

40 + 30   or   80 - 50.

You can sometimes switch numbers around in a math problem to make easy numbers. For example:

3 + 85 + 7 ⟶ (3 + 7) + 85 ⟶ 10 + 85 = 95

or

67 - 12 ⟶ (67 - 10) - 2 ⟶ 57 - 2 = 55

2) Substitute an equal number.

This strategy works especially well with fractions, decimals, and percents.

$\frac{1}{6}$ **x 420 ⟶ 420 ÷ 6** (substitute a whole number for a fraction)

420 ÷ 6 = 70

.25 x 24 ⟶ $\frac{1}{4}$ **x 24** (substitute a fraction for a decimal)

24 ÷ 4 = 6 (substitute a whole number for a fraction)

3) Compensate by changing one or more numbers.

42 + 38 ⟶ (42 + 40) - 2 ⟶ 82 - 2 = 80

$$\begin{array}{r} 376 \\ -\ 98 \\ \end{array}$$ becomes $$\begin{array}{r} 378 \\ -100 \\ \hline 278 \end{array}$$ (raise both numbers by 2)

16

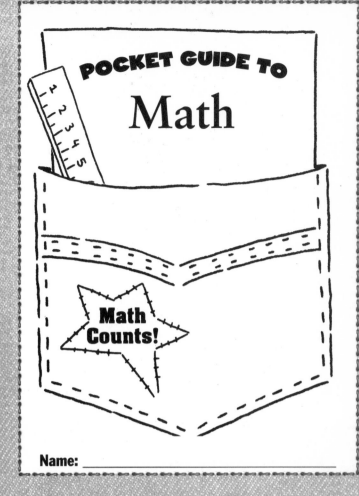

POCKET GUIDE TO
Math

Math Counts!

Name: _____

3

How to Solve Word Problems

When you solve word problems, follow these steps:

1. Read the problem very carefully. Be sure you understand what is being asked. Reread the problem if necessary.
2. Look for clue words. If you see the words *sum*, *total*, *altogether*, or *in all*, you add or multiply. If you see the words *difference*, *how many more*, or *how many less*, you subtract or divide.
3. Decide what you must do (add, subtract, multiply, or divide).
4. Solve the problem.
5. Look at your answer to be sure it makes sense.

| Remember: Some problems may have more than one step. |

Sample Word Problems and Solutions

One-Step Problem

Amy read 10 pages on Monday, 35 pages on Tuesday, and 25 pages on Wednesday. How many pages did she read altogether?

Notice the word *altogether*. This means you need to add.

10 + 35 + 25 = 70

Amy read 70 pages altogether.

14

Table of Contents

Multiplication 4

Division 6

Geometry 8

Tables of Measures 10

Fractions 12

Decimals 13

How to Solve Word Problems 14

Mental Math Tips 16

3

Two-Step Problem

Nate had $50. At the store, he bought a shirt for $10.50 and a hat for $8.25. How much money did he have left?

First, you need to add. → **$10.50 + $8.25 = $18.75**

Then, you need to subtract. → **$50 – 18.75 = $31.25**

Nate had $31.25 left over.

Multi-Step Problem

Nate had $50. At the store, he bought 3 shirts for $10.00 each and 2 belts for $4.50 each. How much money did he have left?

First, you need to multiply. → **3 x $10.00 = $30.00**

2 x $4.50 = $9.00

Then, you need to add → **$30.00 + $9.00 = $39.00**

Finally, you need to subtract. → **$50.00 – $39.00 = $11.00**

Nate had $11.00 left over.

Multiplication

Times Table Chart

To use the table, find the two numbers (or factors) you are multiplying, taking one from the top row and the other from the row along the left side. Now, run your fingers down and across from these numbers. The product will appear where your fingers meet.

X	0	1	2	3	4	5	6	7	8	9
0	0	0	0	0	0	0	0	0	0	0
1	0	1	2	3	4	5	6	7	8	9
2	0	2	4	6	8	10	12	14	16	18
3	0	3	6	9	12	15	18	21	24	28
4	0	4	8	12	16	20	24	28	32	36
5	0	5	10	15	20	25	30	35	40	45
6	0	6	12	18	24	30	36	42	48	54
7	0	7	14	21	28	35	42	49	56	63
8	0	8	16	24	32	40	48	56	64	72
9	0	9	18	27	36	45	54	63	72	81

Decimals

$$4,865.347$$

| thousands | hundreds | tens | ones | tenths | hundredths | thousandths |

Adding Decimals

To add or subtract decimals, be sure the decimal points are lined up, and add or subtract as usual.

$$\begin{array}{r} 14.56 \\ +23.22 \\ \hline 37.78 \end{array}$$

Multiplying Decimals

To multiply, multiply as usual. Then count up the total number of decimal places in your two factors. Your answer must have this many places in it.

$$\begin{array}{r} 3.45 \\ \times\ 2.01 \\ \hline 345 \\ 000 \\ 690 \\ \hline 6.9345 \end{array}$$

Dividing Decimals

Begin dividing decimals the same way you would divide whole numbers.

$$2.5\overline{)40.5}$$

Turn the divisor into a whole number by moving the decimal point. Move the decimal point the same number of places in the dividend.

$$2.5\overline{)40.5}$$

Now divide. Align the decimal point in the quotient with the decimal in the dividend.

$$25\overline{)405.}\quad 16.2$$

Common Equivalents

Fraction	Decimal	Percent
$\frac{1}{2}$	.5	50%
$\frac{1}{3}$	.33	33%
$\frac{1}{5}$	.20	20%
$\frac{1}{4}$	.25	25%
$\frac{1}{8}$	.125	12.5%
$\frac{2}{3}$	.66	66%
$\frac{3}{4}$	.75	75%
$\frac{3}{8}$	.375	37.5%
$\frac{5}{8}$	.625	62.5%
$\frac{7}{8}$	.875	87.5%

Page 48   Quick Reference Guides · Scholastic

Fractions

$\dfrac{4}{5}$ ← numerator (number of parts counted)
← denominator (total parts of the whole or set)

A Few Equivalent Fractions

$$\frac{1}{2} = \frac{2}{4} = \frac{3}{6} = \frac{4}{8} = \frac{5}{10}$$

$$\frac{1}{4} = \frac{2}{8} = \frac{3}{12} = \frac{4}{16} = \frac{5}{20}$$

$$\frac{1}{3} = \frac{2}{6} = \frac{3}{9} = \frac{4}{12} = \frac{5}{15}$$

Multiplying Fractions

To multiply fractions, just multiply the numerator by the numerator, and the denominator by the denominator.

$$\frac{1}{4} \times \frac{1}{8} = \frac{1}{32}$$

Adding and Subtracting Fractions

To add or subtract fractions, the fractions must have common denominators. If the denominators are not the same, you need to convert them to make them the same.

$$\frac{1}{4} + \frac{1}{8} =$$

$$\frac{2}{8} + \frac{1}{8} = \frac{3}{8}$$

$$\frac{5}{6} - \frac{1}{3} =$$

$$\frac{5}{6} - \frac{2}{6} = \frac{3}{6} \text{ or } \frac{1}{2}$$

Dividing Fractions

To divide fractions, you need to flip the divisor fraction and then multiply.

For example, $\dfrac{3}{4} \div \dfrac{1}{4}$

becomes $\dfrac{3}{4} \times \dfrac{4}{1}$

or $\dfrac{12}{4}$ or 3

12

Multi-Digit Multiplication

Here's how to multiply multi-digit numbers.

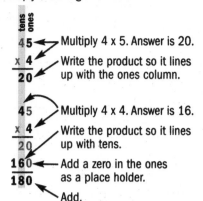

tens ones

45
x 4
—
20 ← Multiply 4 x 5. Answer is 20. Write the product so it lines up with the ones column.

45
x 4
—
20 ← Multiply 4 x 4. Answer is 16. Write the product so it lines up with tens.

160 ← Add a zero in the ones as a place holder.
180 ← Add.

Here is a shorter way to do this problem.

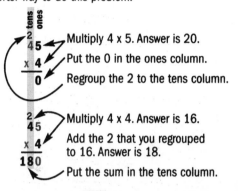

tens ones

2
45
x 4
—
0 ← Multiply 4 x 5. Answer is 20. Put the 0 in the ones column. Regroup the 2 to the tens column.

2
45
x 4
—
180 ← Multiply 4 x 4. Answer is 16. Add the 2 that you regrouped to 16. Answer is 18. Put the sum in the tens column.

5

Tables of Measures

Time

60 seconds = 1 minute
60 minutes = 1 hour
24 hours = 1 day
7 days = 1 week
52 weeks = 1 year
365 days = 1 year
366 days = 1 leap year
12 months = 1 year
10 years = 1 decade
100 years = 1 century
1,000 years = 1 millennium

Length

Standard	Metric
12 inches = 1 foot	10 millimeters = 1 centimeter
3 feet = 1 yard	10 centimeters = 1 decimeter
1,760 yards = 1 mile	10 decimeters = 1 meter
5,280 feet = 1 mile	100 centimeters = 1 meter
	1,000 meters = 1 kilometer

Weight

Standard	Metric
16 ounces = 1 pound	1,000 grams = 1 kilogram
2,000 pounds = 1 ton	1,000 kilograms = 1 metric ton

10

Long Division

When you are dividing numbers with two or more digits, here are the steps you can follow.

$5\overline{)322}$

1. Divide by estimating how many 5s are in 32. If you multiply 6 x 5, you have 30. Write 6 above the 2, and 30 under 32.

$5\overline{)322}$ → quotient 6, 30

2. Subtract 30 from 32. Bring down the 2 in the ones place.

$5\overline{)322}$ → 6, 302, 22

3. Then, divide by estimating how many 5s are in 22. If you multiply 5 x 4, you get 20. Write 4 above the 2, and 20 under 22.

$5\overline{)322}$ → 64 R2, 302, 22, 20, 2

4. You have 2 left. This is your remainder.

Here's a trick for remembering the steps in long division.

Dad	.........Divide
Mom	.........Multiply
Sister	.........Subtract
Brother	.......Bring Down
Rover	.........Remainder

7

Division

dividend	divisor	quotient
56	÷ **7** =	**8**

Here are the division facts you should know in order to divide quickly.

1 ÷ 1 = 1 2 ÷ 1 = 2 3 ÷ 1 = 3 4 ÷ 1 = 4 5 ÷ 1 = 5 6 ÷ 1 = 6 7 ÷ 1 = 7 8 ÷ 1 = 8 9 ÷ 1 = 9	4 ÷ 4 = 1 8 ÷ 4 = 2 12 ÷ 4 = 3 16 ÷ 4 = 4 20 ÷ 4 = 5 24 ÷ 4 = 6 28 ÷ 4 = 7 32 ÷ 4 = 8 36 ÷ 4 = 9	7 ÷ 7 = 1 14 ÷ 7 = 2 21 ÷ 7 = 3 28 ÷ 7 = 4 35 ÷ 7 = 5 42 ÷ 7 = 6 49 ÷ 7 = 7 56 ÷ 7 = 8 63 ÷ 7 = 9
2 ÷ 2 = 1 4 ÷ 2 = 2 6 ÷ 2 = 3 8 ÷ 2 = 4 10 ÷ 2 = 5 12 ÷ 2 = 6 14 ÷ 2 = 7 16 ÷ 2 = 8 18 ÷ 2 = 9	5 ÷ 5 = 1 10 ÷ 5 = 2 15 ÷ 5 = 3 20 ÷ 5 = 4 25 ÷ 5 = 5 30 ÷ 5 = 6 35 ÷ 5 = 7 40 ÷ 5 = 8 45 ÷ 5 = 9	8 ÷ 8 = 1 16 ÷ 8 = 2 24 ÷ 8 = 3 32 ÷ 8 = 4 40 ÷ 8 = 5 48 ÷ 8 = 6 56 ÷ 8 = 7 64 ÷ 8 = 8 72 ÷ 8 = 9
3 ÷ 3 = 1 6 ÷ 3 = 2 9 ÷ 3 = 3 12 ÷ 3 = 4 15 ÷ 3 = 5 18 ÷ 3 = 6 21 ÷ 3 = 7 24 ÷ 3 = 8 27 ÷ 3 = 9	6 ÷ 6 = 1 12 ÷ 6 = 2 18 ÷ 6 = 3 24 ÷ 6 = 4 30 ÷ 6 = 5 36 ÷ 6 = 6 42 ÷ 6 = 7 48 ÷ 6 = 8 54 ÷ 6 = 9	9 ÷ 9 = 1 18 ÷ 9 = 2 27 ÷ 9 = 3 36 ÷ 9 = 4 45 ÷ 9 = 5 54 ÷ 9 = 6 63 ÷ 9 = 7 72 ÷ 9 = 8 81 ÷ 9 = 9

6

Liquid

Standard	Metric
8 fluid ounces = 1 cup	1,000 milliliters = 1 liter
2 cups = 1 pint	1,000 liters = 1 kiloliter
4 cups = 1 quart	
2 pints = 1 quart	
4 quarts = 1 gallon	

Standard Measurement Conversions

Linear
1 inch = 2.54 cm
1 foot = 30.48 cm
1 yard = 0.9144 m
1 mile = 1.609 km
1 centimeter = 0.39 in.
1 meter = 1.09 yd
1 kilometer = 0.62 mi

Weight
1 ounce = 28.35 grams
1 pound = 0.45 kilogram
1 gram = 0.035 ounces
1 kilogram = 2.20 pounds

Volume
1 U.S. gallon = 3.785 liters
1 liter = 0.26 U.S. gallons

Abbreviations

Centimeter	cm	Mile	mi
Foot/Feet	ft	Millimeter	mm
Gallon	gal	Month	mo
Gram	g	Ounce	oz
Hour	hr	Pint	pt
Inch	in.	Pound	lb
Kilogram	kg	Quart	qt
Kilometer	km	Yard	yd
Liter	L	Year	yr
Meter	m		

11

Geometry

Angles

Angles are formed by two rays with a common endpoint.

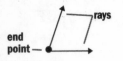

A right angle measures 90°.

An obtuse angle has a measure of more than 90°.

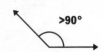

An acute angle has a measure of less than 90°.

Circles

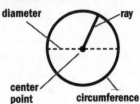

Polygons

Name	Number of Sides & Angles
Triangle	3
Rectangle	4
Quadrilateral	4
Pentagon	5
Hexagon	6
Heptagon	7
Octagon	8
Nonagon	9
Decagon	10

8

Triangles

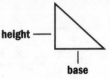

The sum of all the angles of a triangle equals 180°

Right: 1 90° angle
Equilateral: 3 sides of equal length
Isosceles: 2 sides of equal length
Scalene: All 3 sides are of different lengths

Important Formulas

s = side   **b** = base   **h** = height   **l** = length   **w** = width

	Perimeter	Area
Square	4 x **s**	**s** x **s**
Rectangle	2**l** + 2**w**	**l** x **w**
Triangle	**s** + **s** + **s**	$\dfrac{\textbf{b} \times \textbf{h}}{2}$

Circles

Circle circumference: π x d or $2\pi r$.

Area of a circle: πr^2

π (pi) = 3.14

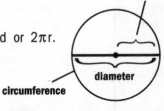

9

Steps of the Scientific Method

1. Base your idea for a science project on an observation.

2. State the purpose of your project. Usually, you will state your purpose in the form of a research question. (For example: Do bigger oranges have bigger seeds than smaller ones?)

3. Do background research to find out what is already known about your topic.

4. State your hypothesis, an educated guess about your research question. (For example: Bigger oranges will have bigger seeds.)

5. Come up with a detailed procedure.

6. Carry out an experiment and collect data.

7. Record the results. In many cases, you can present your results in tables, charts, and graphs.

8. Draw a conclusion from the results. Did your hypothesis prove true?

9. Write down the steps of the procedure and results of your experiment.

10. Publish and present your report.

16

POCKET GUIDE TO
Science

DISCOVER SCIENCE

Name: _____

Weather

Water Cycle

Condensation

Precipitation

Evaporation

Evaporation

Water

Land

14

Table of Contents

Plants 4

Animals 6

Human Body 8

Simple Machines 10

Solar System 12

Weather 14

Steps of the Scientific Method 16

3

Cloud Types

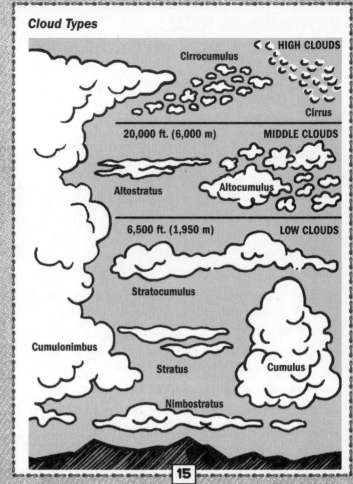

Plants

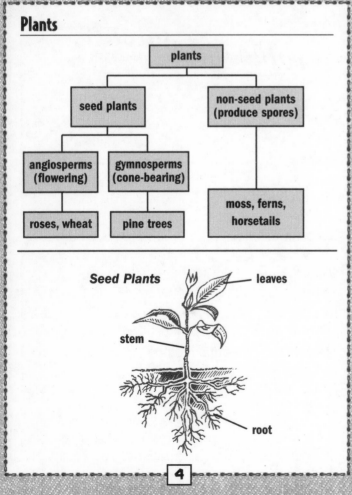

Seed Plants

- leaves
- stem
- root

Here are the planets, listed in size from largest to smallest.	Distance from the Sun (miles)	
	Jupiter	483,780,000
	Saturn	90,750,000
	Uranus	1,784,860,000
	Neptune	2,793,100,000
	Earth	92,960,000
	Venus	67,240,000
	Mars	141,620,000
	Mercury	35,980,000
	Pluto	3,647,240,000

Source: World Book Online

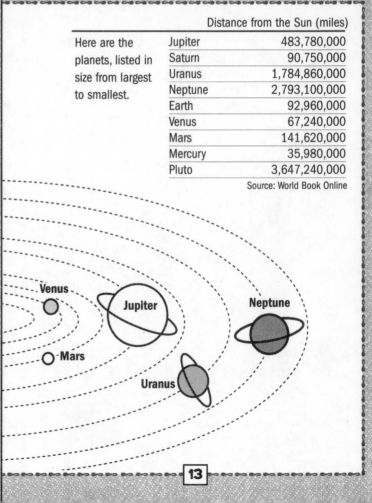

Solar System

The Sun is a huge glowing star mostly made up of hydrogen. Nine planets orbit around the Sun.

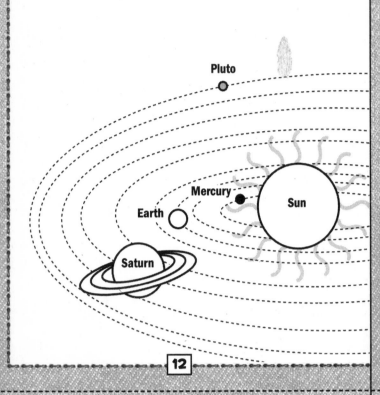

Some seed plants have flowers.
Here are the parts of a flower.

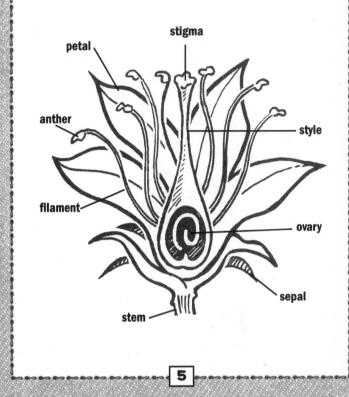

Simple Machines

A simple machine is a tool or device that makes work easier. Here are the five simple machines and how they work.

Lever: A straight rod or board that turns on a fixed point known as the fulcrum. Pushing down on one end of a lever results in the upward motion of the opposite end.

A hammer and bottle opener are examples of a lever.

Pulley: A wheel, usually with a groove around the outside rim to hold a rope in place. Pulling down on the rope can lift an object attached to the rope. Gravity makes it easier to pull down on the rope. A crane and mini-blinds are examples of a pulley.

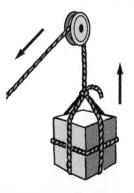

Vertebrates

Animals with backbones are called vertebrates.
Vertebrates can be classified into five different groups.

Group	Characteristics
Fish	scales • breathe through gills • cold-blooded • cartilage or bony skeletons • most lay eggs in water
Amphibians	cold-blooded • moist • scaleless skin • adults have lungs • most lay eggs in water
Reptiles	cold-blooded • dry scales • breathe through lungs • most lay eggs
Birds	warm-blooded • feathers and wings • breathe through lungs • lay eggs
Mammals	warm-blooded • nurse their young • have hair or fur • breathe through lungs • almost all give birth to live young

Animals

There are two major groups of animals: invertebrates and vertebrates.

Invertebrates

Invertebrates are animals without backbones. Spiders, crabs, snails, worms, and lots of other animals are invertebrates.

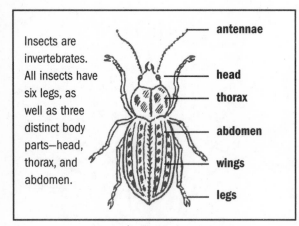

Insects are invertebrates. All insects have six legs, as well as three distinct body parts—head, thorax, and abdomen.

- antennae
- head
- thorax
- abdomen
- wings
- legs

Spiders are not insects. They are a distinct group of invertebrates. All spiders have 8 legs and two body parts.

6

Inclined Plane: An inclined plane has a sloping surface. It is used to change the effort and distance involved in doing work, such as lifting loads. A ramp and a staircase are examples of an inclined plane.

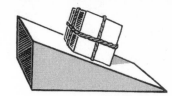

Screw: An inclined plane wrapped around a shaft. The inclined plane allows the screw to move itself or to move an object surrounding it when rotated. A bolt is an example of a screw.

Wheel and Axle: A wheel and axle has a larger wheel connected by a smaller cylinder (axle) that is fastened to the wheel so that they turn together. When the axle is turned, the wheel moves a greater distance than the axle, but less force is needed to move it. The axle moves a shorter distance, but it takes greater force to move it. A steering wheel and a door knob are examples of a wheel and axle.

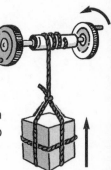

11

Human Body

Here are some of the important parts of the human body.

Skeletal System

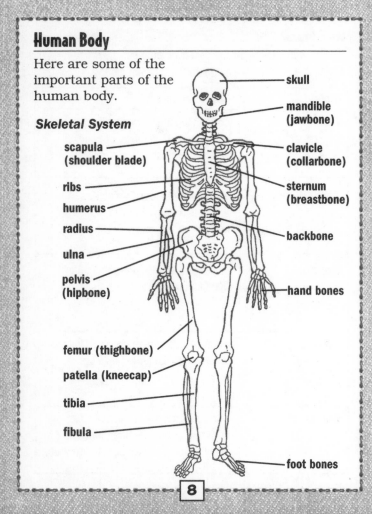

- skull
- mandible (jawbone)
- clavicle (collarbone)
- scapula (shoulder blade)
- sternum (breastbone)
- ribs
- humerus
- radius
- ulna
- backbone
- pelvis (hipbone)
- hand bones
- femur (thighbone)
- patella (kneecap)
- tibia
- fibula
- foot bones

8

Brain

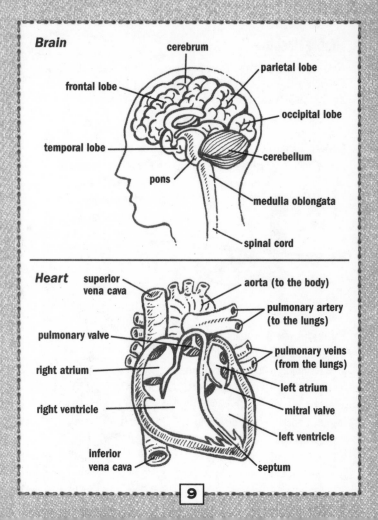

- cerebrum
- parietal lobe
- frontal lobe
- occipital lobe
- temporal lobe
- cerebellum
- pons
- medulla oblongata
- spinal cord

Heart

- superior vena cava
- aorta (to the body)
- pulmonary artery (to the lungs)
- pulmonary valve
- pulmonary veins (from the lungs)
- right atrium
- left atrium
- mitral valve
- right ventricle
- left ventricle
- inferior vena cava
- septum

9

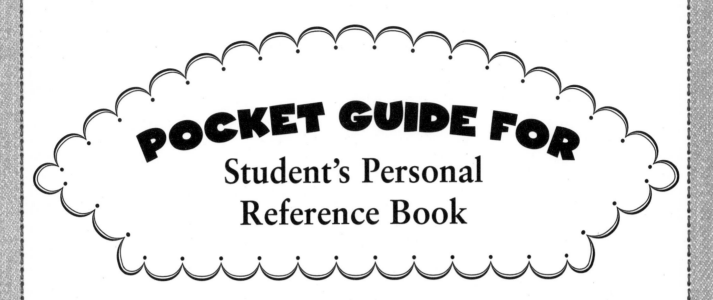

POCKET GUIDE FOR
Student's Personal Reference Book

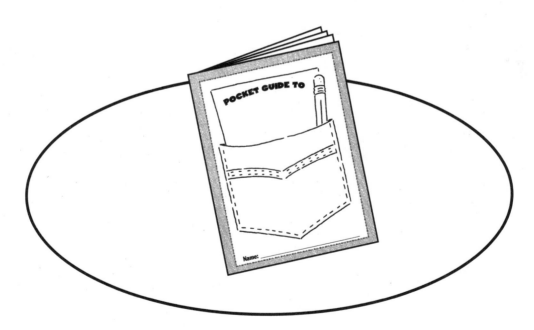

Blank Pocket Guide Template

Invite students to make their own pocket guides using the template on pages 57–60. They might use it to create a study guide for a test or to collect research on a topic. The frames and thought and speech bubbles on pages 61 and 62 can be reproduced for students to paste into their guides.

POCKET GUIDE TO

Name: _____

16

Table of Contents

3

14

2

15

4

13

12

5

10

7

6

11

8

9

Frames & Art

Notes

Notes